A Resilient Heart
From Brokenness to Wholeness

Gwendolyn Scott Clark

OWN LIMIT
SHREVEPORT, LOUISIANA

The opinions expressed in this manuscript are solely the opinions of the author and do not represent the opinions or thoughts of the publisher. The author has represented and warranted full ownership and/or legal right to publish all the materials in this book.

Unless otherwise noted, scripture quotations are taken from the Holy Bible (**Amplified Version**). Definitions referenced from Merriam-Webster On-line Dictionary.

A Resilient Heart
From Brokenness to Wholeness
All Rights Reserved.
Copyright 1999, 2015 Gwendolyn Scott Clark
v2.0

Cover Photo © 2016 thinkstockphotos.com. All rights reserved - used with permission.

This book may not be reproduced, transmitted, or stored in whole or in part by any means, including graphic, electronic, or mechanical without the express written consent of the publisher except in the case of brief quotations embodied in critical articles and reviews.

Own Limit

ISBN: 978-0-692-52779-5

PRINTED IN THE UNITED STATES OF AMERICA

Dedication

This book is dedicated to my son, Jonathan and daughter, Camden.

This book is also dedicated to the loving memory of my father and mother.

And to those who may have past, present, or future experiences with disruptive relationships.

Table of Contents

Acknowledgments v
Preface vi
Introduction vii
Opening Statement viii
Chapter One: A House Divided 1
   Living Together, But Separated 1
Chapter Two: A Christian and Divorced 6
   The State of Divorce 6
   Yielding to God's Power 13
   Forgiveness 15
   ABCs for the Children Experiencing Divorce 19
Chapter Three: Single, Yet Married 23
   Alone, But Not Abandoned 23
   The State of Singleness 26
   A Love Relationship with God 28
Chapter Four: Abundance and Restoration 31
   Lessons Learned 31
   The Neglect of Friendship 32
   Friendship 34
   The Neglect of Intimacy 36
   Intimacy 36
   The Neglect of Courtship 37
   Courtship 38
   The Neglect of Marriage 40
   Marriage 42
   He Restores My Soul 46
   Reunited 50
Reflections 54
About the Author 57

Acknowledgments

Honor and Praises are given to the Lord Jesus Christ, Who has given me the inspiration and knowledge to express my thoughts with words and to use His word as a reference. He has been my counselor every step of the way!

To my family and friends: thank you for the encouragement, support, and prayers.

Abundance of thanks to and showers of blessings upon my son, Jonathan and daughter, Camden: you both have been remarkable in sharing your love and support throughout the years.

A Special thanks to my pastor Bishop Fred A. Caldwell, Sr., First Lady Mary K. Caldwell, and the Greenwood Acres Full Gospel Baptist Church Family. I am most grateful that God saw fit to place me in a teaching ministry of great merit. Because it has played, and continues to play, a vital role in structuring, inspiring, and motivating me to keep moving forward, both during and after my disruptive relationship experience.

Preface

When faced with trials, tribulations, and devastating circumstances, one must possess inner fortitude to move forward with life. Therefore, **A Resilient Heart** is needed to survive. This heart can only come by embracing God and allowing His word to heal the brokenness and replace it with wholeness.

Introduction

> **Above all else guard your heart, for everything you do flows from it. Proverbs 4:23 (NIV)**

At times, situations and circumstances can come upon us without warning, as it seems. Literally, they can knock us to our knees and sometimes lay us flat on our backs. When this occurs, remember two key facts. One, we must be able to recover from shock and devastation. Two, we must be able to become strong again and bounce back from the experience.

With this in mind, the inner aspect of every human (combination of the soul and spirit) is where the heart (life source) lies, and just like the physical human heart, both are vital to our existence.

To define, **A Resilient Heart** is a heart that can withstand or recover quickly from difficulty or devastating circumstances.

Opening Statement

While married in my early twenties, the majority of events in this book occurred closer to my latter twenties. I was brought up in the church from birth, and joined the Methodist church at age twelve. But really had a born again experience in my latter twenties at year three of my six and a half year marriage.

My former spouse and I experienced divorce as Christians. However, we were not mature in our Christian walk and ignorant about matters of marriage. That is to say, we had not renewed our minds with the word of God in how we should conduct ourselves overall in life as well as in a marital relationship.

Reflecting back, I realize that we both played significant roles in the disruption of the relationship. This book is not meant to shed any negative connotation on anyone's character, speaker included. Nevertheless, being honest can reveal error and weakness. For this reason, one fact remains true; if there is a desire to change, then change can happen. And you can live beyond pain, hurt, and disruptive relationships; no matter the contributing factors.

CHAPTER

A House Divided

Living Together, But Separated

THERE ARE MANY couples in the body of Christ who are living in a pretentious state; some hold offices or leadership positions in the church. My former spouse and I were one of those couples. We were living together at the same physical address. However, we never really shared the others' interests, dreams, or thoughts; there was no friendship or intimacy. We worked in the church, but did not put in the work that was truly needed at home, with one another. Basically, we did not know how to live together as husband and wife. For the majority of the marriage we were living together, but separated. We did get along, but we lived outside of a happy marriage. Because for us; it did not exist.

When we were in public view, we were perceived as being together by others. But when we were at home, we were basically seeing one another in passing, with little to no communication. We simply displayed or put up this front of togetherness. Our living arrangements became similar to that of roommates. For example, going in and out of the home daily; merely existing.

Usually, when there is little to no communication or togetherness, it represents separation. Therefore, we never lived together mentally or spiritually. Though we were married, we did not develop the **"oneness"** that continues to be cultivated after marriage. To explain, I am referring to the **"oneness"** that creates the **"one flesh"**, which is developed when the two individuals start to mind the same things and come on one accord mentally and emotionally. As a result, they can walk together spiritually. Surely, to achieve this, will take effort and work. At the same time, from a Christian perspective, we must see marriage as an investment that appreciates over time. In other words, what you put in as a deposit will eventually produce growth or increase.

> *[6]But from the beginning of the creation God made them male and female. [7]For this cause shall a man leave [behind] his father and mother and be joined to his wife and cleave closely to her permanently. [8]And the two shall become one flesh, so that they are no longer two, but one flesh.* **Mark 10:6-8**

Married, but living separated in the home does not honor God. Furthermore, **"How can we lead in the church?"** Scripture tells us that before we can take care of the things of God we need to first take care of our own things. **How can we become committed to God's house and not committed to our own house?** First and foremost, God should be able to see our faithfulness at home with our spouse, whom He has entrusted in our care. And then He can trust us to be faithful with a pure heart in His kingdom work.

For instance, what we display in public as Christian couples should also be displayed at home with one another. We must be **true** to ourselves as well as one another. Above all, God desires truth, and that truth to be in the inward parts. As a couple, we cannot stand against the attacks of Satan and utilize the power and strength of the marital union, unless we stand together in agreement. For this reason, there is no place for division in the Christian marriage or household.

> *And if a house is divided (split into factions and rebelling) against itself, that house will not be able to last.* **Mark 3:25**

> *For if a man does not know how to rule his own household, how is*

he to take care of the church of God? **1Timothy 3:5**

Behold, You desire truth in the inner being; make me therefore to know wisdom in my inmost heart. **Psalm 51:6**

Do two walk together except they make an appointment and have agreed? **Amos 3:3**

Being married means that two individuals have come together to become united in a partnership for life. They both bring differences, strengths, and weaknesses. However, God uniquely designed us to follow the pattern of opposites attract. We are to compliment or enhance one another's differences, strengths, and weaknesses. This can only happen effectively if we allow God to guide us, and show us our spouse's needs and how we should minister to them.

I struggled with many feelings of insecurity in my marriage and my emotions controlled me. I felt as if I needed my former spouse to constantly have the right actions or say the right words to keep me feeling secure in the marriage. I literally placed unrealistic expectations upon him and caused him to feel frustrated and manipulated.

Generally speaking, your spouse has the right to express their own feelings and identity. However, my former spouse had a quiet, reserved personality. This displayed submissiveness and allowed me to be in control. I would estimate that he would agree ninety-five percent of the time to my suggestions or plans. And when I voiced my opinion, I did it with a condescending attitude. And because of this, we both shared so much suppressed anger and resentment in regards to these behaviors.

Subsequently, I realized that the anger and resentment I felt was due to his submissive role. And because he did not take responsibility of the leadership role in our marriage, not to mention, as the head of me; our roles in the marriage became reversed and did not reflect God's order. Whenever we alter God's order, we give birth to strife and many other behaviors and attitudes that are not pleasing to Him.

To put it another way, our words and behaviors were a result of immaturity. I was ignorant to the fact that we were giving place to

A RESILIENT HEART

the enemy and had opened the door to create a brutal stabbing wound in both of us that eventually led to the destruction of the marriage. Retrospectively, this was a silent killer of the relationship.

In the long run, for us to have victory in marriage, we must follow God's order. We must keep our marital relationships real and give our spouses room for error. The fact remains that no man or woman is without error.

> *²²Wives, be subject (be submissive and adapt yourselves) to your own husbands as [a service] to the Lord. ²³For the husband is head of the wife as Christ is the Head of the church, Himself the Savior of [His] body.* **Ephesians 5:22-23**

> *Death and life are in the power of the tongue, and they who indulge in it shall eat the fruit of it [for death or life].* **Proverbs 18:21**

> *⁵Even so the tongue is a little member and it can boast of great things. See how much wood or how great a forest a tiny spark can set a blaze! ⁸But the human tongue can be tamed by no man. It is a restless (undisciplined, irreconcilable) evil, full of deadly poison. ⁹With it we bless the Lord and Father, and with it we curse men who are made in God's likeness! ¹⁰Out of the same mouth come forth blessings and cursing. These things, my brethren, ought not to be so.* **James 3: 5, 8-10**

Furthermore, I did not understand who I was in Christ, neither my role as a wife, as relates to the word of God. But now, I realize that my security and completeness is in Christ. And understand that I must allow the word of God to renew my mind in regards to marriage and my role as a wife. Therefore, as we come into an understanding of His word, and begin to practice it, God can then mature us in our words and behaviors. Still, we have to make an individual choice to want to put away certain immature conversation and behaviors; and truly desire genuine change. As we participate and begin to function in our God-ordained roles as husband and wife, we will maintain God's proper order for marriage. When this occurs, the word of God can work and the results will be that of maturity and peace in the home.

> *When I was a child, I talked like a child, I thought like a child, I reasoned like a child, now that I have become a man, I am done with childish ways and have put them aside.* **1 Corinthians 13:11**

> *For we all stumble and fall and offend in many things. And if anyone does not offend in speech [never says wrong things], he is a fully developed character and a perfect man, able to control his whole body to curb his entire nature.* **James 3:2**

CHAPTER *Two*

A Christian and Divorced

The State of Divorce

IN THIS CHAPTER, I will share my experience with divorce as a Christian and how it affected my life. All things considered, everyone's situation is different in the specifics, but the general principles and overall experience of divorce is the same. Unfortunately, divorce happens to many people, Christians and non-Christians alike. However, today Christians are divorcing one another at alarming rates and **Christians** seem to think that it is okay to seek this type of resolution for their marital problems. On the contrary, there is a better solution than divorce for the Christian marriage. All things being equal, the solution is found in the word of God, and that solution is reconciliation.

    I am not condemning anyone who has been or at this very moment going through a divorce, but I am saying that God's plan for marriage is not divorce. God is not an advocate of divorce, He hates it. But, He loves divorcees. Even though I was not the one initiating the divorce, I still had to repent before God and my spouse of any area or areas in the marriage that I had fallen short, whether by omission or commission. And at that point, I received forgiveness, and asked God to reveal to me those areas where I needed change. Ordinarily, this is done so we will not make the same mistakes in the future.

For all have sinned, and come short of the glory of God; **Romans 3:23 (KJV)**

[10] But to the married people I give charge—not I but the Lord—that the wife is not to separate from her husband. [11] But if she does [separate from and divorce him], let her remain single or else be reconciled to her husband. And [I charge] the husband [also] that he should not put away or divorce his wife. **1 Corinthians 7:10-11**

[13] And this you do with double guilt; you cover the altar of the Lord with tears [shed by you unoffending wives, divorced by you that you might take heathen wives], and with [your own] weeping and crying out because the Lord does not regard your offering any more or accept it with favor at your hand. [14] Yet you ask, Why does He reject it? Because the Lord was witness [to the covenant made at your marriage] between you and the wife of your youth, against whom you have dealt treacherously and to whom you were faithless. Yet she is your companion and the wife of your covenant [made by your marriage vows]. [15] And did not God make [you and your wife one [flesh]? Did not One make you and preserve your spirit alive? And why [did God make you two] one? Because He sought a godly offspring [from your union]. Therefore take heed to yourselves, and let no one deal treacherously and be faithless to the wife of his youth. [16] For the Lord, the God of Israel, says: I hate divorce and marital separation and him who covers his garment [his wife] with violence. Therefore keep a watch upon your spirit [that it may be controlled by My Spirit], and that you deal not treacherously and faithlessly [with your marriage mate]. **Malachi 2:13-16**

Let me give an illustration on when divorce actually occurs and how we can recognize that fact. Generally, divorce occurs when one spouse (or both) puts the other away; not just a physical act of moving away and not living at the same address. However, this is a mental act; a feeling of disinterest.

For the most part, the putting away actually occurs long before any court appearance has taken place or any legal document is final. To explain, **"to be put away"** is defined as: there is no acknowledgement of the others' presence, no respect shown to them, no communication with them, and basically no regard for them in any affectionate way. You become estranged, and there is no emotional closeness or intimacy, you become mentally unattached from the other person. You are totally disinterested.

Let me point out, the reasons for the occurrence of any divorce may vary with individual circumstances. Basically, our reasons were that my former spouse was disinterested with me as well as the marriage, and believed that he could do better and have more in life with someone else, and there was an absence of love towards me.

During this time my focus was to receive marital counseling and trying to work out any differences we may have had; I only believed since we were Christians there was nothing that we should not be able to work out with God's help. At that point, I tried to prove to him and to myself that I would change or do whatever it took to convince him to change his mind and make the marriage work. However, he did not feel the same way. I had to remind myself that another person's will was involved and I only had control over my will and actions. With this in mind, I realized three key facts about divorce and will point them out in the following paragraphs.

One, divorce is a spirit. And it attaches itself to people as a mindset that encourages their will to become contrary to the will of God, as relates to marriage. This mindset influences them to see divorce as the best way out. So, they allow their emotions or feelings to control them. It becomes a stronghold and this develops into a hardened heart. For example, if a man's heart becomes hardened as a result of their thinking process and that process becomes very difficult to penetrate. Usually, this occurs when your spouse has come to a decision about you, how they feel about the marriage, and that divorce is their solution and the only way out. They only believe that their way of thinking is correct and everyone else is wrong. They are unwilling to hear what God's word says about divorce. They are unwilling to discuss any type of reconciliation. And no amount of persuasion, reasoning, or truth shared with them will make a difference. They believe what they believe and that is it!

To define, hardness of heart is the unwillingness to acknowledge the truth or to show resistance to what is the truth. And this is a weapon, as relates to divorce that is used by Satan to destroy God's plan for marriage.

Jesus addressed the issue of man's hardness of heart with the Pharisees in **Mark 10:2-5**. To paraphrase, the Pharisees wanted to trick Jesus with the question they were asking Him. In brief, they really wanted to justify why it was okay to divorce, because after all they said, Moses allowed it. And Jesus came back and told the Pharisees, Moses told them to divorce because they had heartened their hearts. To put it another way, "Go ahead and do it, because you have already made up your mind and nothing that I can say or try to reason with you at this point will sway your opinion or thoughts about divorce". In summary, see it was not that divorce was okay, it was in their minds and their wills were set to act on it. Therefore, the condition of their heart was influenced by their thoughts, their will, and their emotions and it became settled for them at that point. So, Jesus clarified the reason Moses allowed divorce, not because God was in agreement with divorce or that it was okay to do it; it was because of their decision that it was allowed.

> *²As some Pharisees came up, and, in order to test Him and try to find a weakness in Him, asked, Is it lawful for a man to dismiss and repudiate and divorce his wife? ³He answered them, What did Moses command you? ⁴They replied, Moses allowed a man to write a bill of divorce and put her away. ⁵But Jesus said to them, Because of your hardness of heart [your condition of insensibility to the call of God] he wrote you this precept in your Law.* **Mark 10:2-5**

Two, divorce is an upheaval of life. It is confusion, deception, division, and pain. There are no words that are known to man that can adequately describe the hurt, pain, and torment that occurs within the human soul after a divorce occurs. It disrupts the lives of the children, relatives, and friends of the two parties involved. All these people are generally placed in awkward positions and no longer can relate to either of the parties as they have in the past. Divorce causes past friendships to end. Basically, a sense of loyalty seems to have been betrayed when either friend communicates with one person and not the other. On the negative side, I lost many friendships and many relatives became distant. I had to learn how to love those people from a distance, and over time God gave me the strength to do it.

Three, divorce is considered as being unfaithful (faithless), not honoring a commitment, breaking a vow (or covenant), and basically, not honoring your word. In the institution of the Christian marriage, we are obligated to deter divorce from ever occurring, if at all possible. However, if we should find ourselves in the state of divorce; the first action to take is to seek counsel from God. And receive inner peace that He has spoken to your heart concerning the situation. Also, believe that He will continually guide you as to what you need to do for your specific situation. Granted, the first action to take in any marital situation is to seek God.

Nonetheless, as Christians, when we don't seek God, but allow our minds to drift, and begin to meditate in our thoughts about what we lack with our spouse. Immediately, we start to focus on our thoughts and feelings and begin to establish certain facts in our minds. Such as, our spouse can no longer bring us excitement or happiness. This type of thought will lead to feelings of discontentment and restlessness, and create an appetite to want more and to search for something or someone different or new. That is to say, our spouse no longer appeals to our mental as well as our physical senses. In fact, one or both spouses may become detached, passive, or bored. This is called disinterest. And it will open the door for the enemy and trouble. Without question, this is what happened to me.

We must be realistic and understand that depending on where our maturity level is during the various stages of a marriage (newlywed, early years, middle years, and senior years) and as time progresses, each individual in the marital relationship will change, whether mentally, physically, or spiritually. Also, unexpected challenges and situations may arise. And when these occur, there is a need to have in place a solid foundation that can stand against change and adversity. Ultimately, that foundation is

Jesus Christ, the glue that keeps the Christian marriage together and without Him divorce is imminent.

I recognized (even though my former spouse did not recognize) that disinterest is a very deceptive tactic of Satan and one of his age old lies, which may lead to many divorces in the body of Christ. And this should not be. Because the enemy will always make things seem so much more enticing and better on the outside than they look on the inside. The world knows this concept as: **"the grass is greener on the other side"**. Probably, many of us can agree this cliché is not true.

Nevertheless, this cliché as well as being drawn away by our own lusts and passions, has gotten many people into numerous regretful situations. Even back in the Garden of Eden, when Eve allowed that serpent of old to beguile her. Obviously, she already had abundance in what God had given her in the Garden. However, the serpent wanted to peak her curiosity into thinking she needed more or make her believe that God was withholding something from her. So, she took the bait of the serpent's enticing words, and allowed her feelings (emotions) to dominate, and she ate from the tree of knowledge of good and evil. Eve perceived that the fruit was good. Her eyes saw it. It looked good. And it appealed to her senses. Therefore, she desired it. She wanted it. So she acted upon her feelings and it brought her trouble, and all those associated with her for generations to come. It must be remembered, that when we make decisions (good or bad), their outcomes can affect others, not just ourselves. And some outcomes last for generations.

> *[1]Now the serpent was more subtle and crafty than any living creature of the field which the Lord God had made. And he [Satan] said to the woman, Can it really be that God said, You shall not eat from every tree of the garden? [2]And the woman said to the serpent, We may eat the fruit from the trees of the garden, [3]Except the fruit from the tree which is in the middle of the garden. God has said, You shall not eat of it, neither shall you touch it, lest you die. [4]But the serpent said to the woman, you shall not surely die, [5]For God knows that in the day you eat of it your eyes will be opened, and*

> *you will be like God, knowing the difference between good and evil and blessing and calamity. ⁶And when the woman saw that the tree was good (suitable, pleasant) for food and that it was delightful to look at, and a tree to be desired in order to make one wise, she took of its fruit and ate; and gave some also to her husband, and he ate. ¹³And the Lord God said to the woman, What is this you have done? And the woman said, The serpent beguiled (cheated, outwitted, and deceived) me, and I ate.* **Genesis 3:1-6, 13**

> *But every person is tempted when he is drawn away, enticed and baited by his own evil desire (lust, passions).* **James 1:14**

Above all, when we find ourselves drifting from our spouse, as Christians, we need to humble ourselves before God and seek Him for guidance. Be aware and remember that **"the grass is not always greener on the other side"** and that **"we have what we need in our own spouse"**. If we are not happy or satisfied with how the relationship is going, we should first do a self-assessment and work on our individual selves. Then we can go to our spouse and communicate our needs and desires that we would like to see improve, and be patient with one another as well as the process of growth.

> *If any of you is deficient in wisdom, let him ask of the giving God [Who gives] to everyone liberally and ungrudgingly, without reproaching or faultfinding, and it will be given him.* **James 1:5**

When the divorce actually became final legally, my will would not allow me to embrace it as truth or reality, so mentally I could not receive it as final. That is to say, the divorce was final legally and I had the paperwork in hand to prove it. However, I struggled with wanting my marriage to work. It literally consumed my thoughts and caused me to grieve for a long period of time after the divorce. After months of feeling this way, I picked up the paperwork and read it thoroughly and was shaken quickly into reality. Immediately, it hit home mentally that I was the rejected spouse and that the divorce was true and real. I found myself left with many negative emotions such as, feelings of lovelessness, abandonment, and low self-esteem.

I continually asked myself many questions such as: **"Where do I go from here?" "What kind of life would I have?" "Would future dreams and hopes for my children and I still come true?" "Would anyone ever love me genuinely?"** All these thoughts and many more entered my mind. However, the major question at that moment was: **"How am I ever going to pick up the broken pieces of my heart and live again?"** Well, I found the answer to that question. And it involved my decision to make a conscious effort to choose life, instead of death. To get back up and live again.

For example, the choice of life was to believe God and His promise of life and the choice of death was to believe the lie that the circumstances that surrounded me were leading me into an unproductive, unfulfilled life as my final outcome.

With this in mind, I chose to believe God and His promise which was life and that I could have life more abundantly. His promise; included that He would heal my brokenness and replace it with wholeness, and later experience a life of abundance and restoration. I could not allow the enemy to steal any more from me. So immediately, I had to take control of my thoughts and believe God's promises above my circumstances. I had to renew my mind with the word of God and focus on His promises for me.

> *The thief comes only in order to steal and kill and destroy. I came that they may have and enjoy life, and have it in abundance (to the full, till it overflows).* **John 10:10**

> *Casting down imaginations, and every high thing that exalteth itself against the knowledge of God, and bringing into captivity every thought to the obedience of Christ;* **2 Corinthians 10:5 (KJV)**

Yielding to God's Power

As stated earlier, the decision of divorce was not mine. On the contrary, I had to accept the fact that it had occurred in my spouse's heart and mind. I had to by faith, submit my will to accept that fact. I made a decision to speak life to myself and my circumstances saying, **"I refuse to**

allow this situation of divorce to take me under". "I am getting over this and it is going to make me better and stronger than I've ever been in my life". "I have Jesus on my side and He is my help and source for everything". These confessions became my mantra. Therefore, I chose to believe God to restore all that I had lost.

> *Death and life are in the power of the tongue, and they who indulge in it shall eat the fruit of it [for death or life].* **Proverbs 18:21**

> *And I will restore or replace for you the years that the locust has eaten— the hopping locust, the stripping locust, and the crawling locust, My army which I sent among you.* **Joel 2:25**

> *According to his divine power hath given us all things that pertain unto life and godliness, through the knowledge of him that hath called us to glory and virtue:* **2 Peter 1:3 (KJV)**

When I acknowledged my brokenness and the need to improve myself; I opened my heart and my life to God. As a result, the Holy Spirit revealed areas where change was needed and once again, I began to renew my mind with the word of God. See, the fact remains, we all can change if we are willing to put forth the effort and cooperate with God. That is to say, the human will must be submissive, the human heart (the inner aspect of man) must be receptive, and the life of the individual must be committed to obeying what the word of God says above anything else. Then change becomes imminent after yielding to His power and authority, which is the word of God. And only by renewing our minds with His word, will we see permanent changes in our lives that cannot be altered. Because when the word of God changes us, it changes our heart (the inner aspect of man) and creates permanent results in our daily lives. This produces a lifestyle change. In fact, whenever God does a work, it is forever.

> *For we are God's [own] handiwork (His workmanship), recreated in Christ Jesus, [born anew] that we may do those good works which God predestined (planned beforehand) for us [taking paths*

which He prepared ahead of time], that we should walk in them [living the good life which He prearranged and made ready for us to live]. **Ephesians 2:10**

He is the sole expression of the glory of God [the Light-being, the out-raying or radiance of the divine], and He is the perfect imprint and very image of [God's] nature, upholding and maintaining, and guiding and propelling the universe by His mighty word of power. **Hebrews 1:3a**

I know that whatever God does, it endures forever; nothing can be added to it nor anything taken from it. And God does it so that men will [reverently] fear Him [revere and worship Him, knowing that He is]. **Ecclesiastes 3:14**

Forgiveness

To forgive someone is a conscious act of one's will. It is a choice, not based on emotions or how we feel about the situation or the individual who offended us. In this case, I made the decision to forgive my former spouse for all the hurtful words spoken and any unkind deeds done to me during the marriage, separation, and divorce. See, if I allow unforgiveness to be active in my life, I hinder my prayers and the word of God from working in my life to change my situation. Furthermore, I will be held captive in my soul (mind, will, and emotions). Not to mention, if there remains unforgiveness, envy, strife, and hatred in my heart that I have not dealt with concerning another individual, then this provides an entry for the enemy to work or create torment in my life. There is a bondage that unforgiveness brings because of our refusal to acknowledge the feeling of unforgiveness and emotional imbalances. Also, unforgiveness can hinder me from moving forward to experience emotional healing and restoration.

There were many times, I thought I was really walking in forgiveness toward my former spouse. Instead, as time progressed, I came to the realization that I was still upset and angry and felt that he needed to pay for all the pain and hurt that I was experiencing.

In addition, I believed if I forgave him he would be getting off the hook, and that was not fair in my eyes. This was the wrong attitude and it did not line up with God's word. In the same way, there are many people connected to our lives when we experience divorce that also hurt us, intentionally as well as unintentionally. Because of this, I found myself having to forgive more than my former spouse. After all, I would have to release everyone and let them go and allow God to do what only He could do, and that was to recompense or repay me for the loss and hurt I had experienced.

On the positive side, to illustrate what happens in our lives when we choose to forgive, let's look at Job's reaction to his friends with their judgmental and accusing attitudes. To paraphrase, Job's friends betrayed him with their words and actions in his time of need. Nevertheless, God blessed Job after he prayed for them.

> *And the Lord turned the captivity of Job and restored his fortunes, when he prayed for his friends; also the Lord gave Job twice as much as he had before.* **Job 42:10**

Accordingly, I prayed for my former spouse and all those who offended, hurt, or betrayed me. Regardless of what they said, or did to me during the separation and divorce. I continually prayed for them and myself. At this point, I sincerely came into the knowledge of the truth that I needed to make my confession to forgive. I needed to obey God so my prayers would not be hindered. This was not easy, because my flesh wanted to stay there and feel justified. But I stepped out in faith and obeyed God's word. I totally surrendered my feelings and my will unto God so He could help me truly forgive everyone; then He strengthened me, and gave me the grace I needed to keep His commandments concerning forgiveness.

Significantly, this was to my advantage because it released me to move forward with life and allowed God to begin the process to heal the brokenness.

Judge not [neither pronouncing judgment nor subjecting to censure], and you will not be judged; do not condemn and pronounce guilty; and you will not be condemned and pronounced guilty; acquit and forgive and release (give up resentment, let it drop), and you will be acquitted and forgiven and released. **Luke 6:37**

Pay attention and always be on your guard [looking out for one another]. If your brother sins (misses the mark), solemnly tell him so and reprove him, and if he repents (feel sorry for having sinned), forgive him. **Luke 17:3**

And Jesus prayed, Father, forgive them, for they know not what they do. **Luke 23:34a**

And become useful and helpful and kind to one another, tenderhearted, (compassionate, understanding, loving-hearted), forgiving one another [readily and freely], as God in Christ forgave you. **Ephesians 4:32**

[21]Then Peter came up to Him and said, Lord, how many times may my brother sin against me and I forgive him and let it go? [As many as] up to seven times? [22]Jesus answered him, I tell you, not up to seven times, but seventy times seven! **Matthew 18:21-22**

Be gentle and forbearing with one another and, if one has a difference (a grievance or complaint) against another, readily pardoning each other; even as the Lord has [freely] forgiven you, so must you also [forgive]. **Colossians 3:13**

[23]Therefore is the kingdom of heaven likened unto a certain king, which would take into account of his servants. [24]And when he had begun to reckon, one was brought unto him, which ought (owed) him ten thousand talents. [25]But forasmuch as he had not to pay, his lord commanded him to be sold, and his wife, and children, and all that he had, and payment to be made. [26]The servant therefore fell down, and worshipped him, saying, Lord,

have patience with me, and I will repay thee all. ²⁷Then the lord of the servant was moved with compassion, and loosed him, and forgave him the debt. ²⁸But the same servant went out, and found one of his fellowservants, which owed him an hundred pence: and laid hands on him, and took him by the throat saying, Pay me that thou owest. ²⁹And his fellowservant fell down at his feet, and besought him, saying, Have patience with me, and I will pay thee all. ³⁰And he would not; but went and cast him into prison, till he should pay the debt.³¹So when the fellowservants saw what was done, they were very sorry, and came and told unto their lord all that was done. ³²Then his lord, after that he had called him, said unto him, O thou wicked servant, I forgave thee all that debt, because thou desiredst me: ³³Shouldest not thou also have had compassion on thy fellowservant, even as I had pity on thee? ³⁴And his lord was wroth, and delivered him to the tormentors, till he should pay all that was due unto him. ³⁵So likewise shall my heavenly Father do also unto you, if ye from your hearts forgive not everyone his brother their trespasses. **Matthew 18:23-35 (KJV)**

If I regard iniquity in my heart, the Lord will not hear me; **Psalm 66:18**

Beloved, never avenge yourselves, but leave the way open for [God's] wrath: for it is written, Vengeance is Mine, I will repay (requite), says the Lord. **Romans 12:19**

For we know Him Who said, Vengeance is Mine [retribution and the meting out of full justice rest with Me]; I will repay [I will exact the compensation], says the Lord. And again, The Lord will judge and determine and solve and settle the cause and the cases of His people. **Hebrews 10:30**

And forgive us our debts, as we also have forgiven (left, remitted, and let go of the debts, and have given up resentment against) our debtors. **Matthew 6:12**

ABCs for the Children Experiencing Divorce

In some instances, a child or children may have lived with the knowledge of their parents living together and being married for years, then later have to accept them as divorced. Our children were young, ages two and one when the separation occurred and ages three and almost two when the divorce became legally final. Divorce is very upsetting to the children involved, regardless of their age. For this reason, there were many concerns I had regarding my children and their experience with divorce. Later to find, that each child will experience many phases of adjustment, and at varying degrees and times during the separation and divorce.

Furthermore, when divorce occurs, children should not be made to feel as if they are a statistic, the marriage became the statistic when it ended in divorce; not the children.

From day one, I took the responsibility as a Christian parent to convey to my children the fact that in spite of the negative circumstances of divorce that the family may have experienced, they could succeed and be fulfilled in life, by allowing Christ to fill the voids they may feel as a result of the divorce.

In general, the feelings of emptiness, loneliness, and low self-esteem can be used as avenues or traps (in the form of people or worldly, material things) that the enemy will use to steal their God-given destiny. I had to be there for them, and create a positive, loving environment so God could teach me how to mold them. And keep them on the path that He desired for them.

There were two initial things I did to help make the transition smooth for my children. One, I sought help, and allowed God to guide me in the path that I should follow for my children. Two, I was respectful and truthful about the circumstances and events that occurred concerning the divorce when talking to them. As a general rule, this will cultivate trust and respect in the way they see you and their perception of the divorce.

Generally speaking, when divorce occurs the children may face some or all of these situations:

- Not being able to see one parent on a daily basis

- Not having the flexibility to call and talk to the other parent, especially if they have remarried and have other family obligations

- Feeling a sense of something is wrong with me when other peers at school may talk about activities that they do at home with a mom and dad present

- Longing to be with the parent that they are not living with especially when they want to escape discipline

- Wanting you to give them more attention and affirmation for the void they feel because they miss the other parent

- Hearing negative comments or seeing negative actions and gestures from one parent when speaking to them about the other parent

The **ABCs** during and after divorce are three basic concepts I used to help my children and guide them forward in life:

A-Attention was given and shown to them by putting my primary focus on them and spending quality time with them, not on any other relationships, especially those with the opposite sex and trying to become involved with dating. During this time I was dedicated and committed to making their life successful. Meanwhile, I decided to trust God for the outcome of my life, and I had to remind myself continually that I was investing in and planting seeds into the lives of my children because they are the future generation and my legacy.

B-Build in them a positive self-esteem and affirm them. Focusing on the positive aspects of their personalities and talents. I kept them active with family functions as well as church and school activities. This provided positive support systems, and helped to develop their communication and social skills.

C- Communicate Christ to them; I kept them in a bible-based church and sought help from my pastor and others when I needed counsel in regards to them. And continually demonstrated love to them by my words as well as my actions. Giving them that daily tangible example of Christ. I spoke positive words to them and over their lives.

> *Train up a child in the way he should go [and in keeping with his individual gift or bent], and when he is old he will not depart from it.* **Proverbs 22:6**

With these concepts in mind, I explained things to my children using age appropriate terms and discernment of what details and how much information that I needed to give them; I anticipated, as time progressed they would have more questions. Typically, they will see and hear the actions and opinions of family, friends, and others concerning their parents and what may have occurred between them.

For the most part, family, friends, and others may have various ideas, opinions, and skepticism when it concerns the topics of family, marriage, and divorce. As a matter of fact, people will always offer their opinions. Especially, when they have not themselves had any experience with that type of situation. Occasionally, people can be very cruel at the most inopportune times.

Besides, family, marriage, and divorce are controversial topics, and everyone's opinions are not based upon biblical principles. Therefore, I had to be aware that my children would face those who were not born again or those who may be born again, but minds were not renewed (they would be carnal minded). So, when there was a need to explain, I had to be ready to share with them why I had inner hope, despite the circumstances. And give my children honest, truthful answers based on biblical principles, as relates to the events before, during, and after the divorce.

Although talking to them is very important, there is something that is of equal importance, if not more important; and that is to lead by example. Taking this into consideration, I began to think back when I was eleven years old and remembering what I saw and learned. During that time in my life, I saw one of my sisters go through a separation with her husband because of physical abuse. I learned a lot from her example about forgiveness, and how to provide a positive environment for a child. My sister never said negative things about the situation, my brother-in-law, or his family to my nephew.

Throughout the years, she was always cordial to him and his family, even to the point of maintaining relationships with many of them. I saw her as a great role model. Therefore, her example influenced me tremendously to use this as the foundation on how I needed to monitor and protect my children and lead by example.

All things considered, children learn from social interactions and assess their surroundings by observation and listening in great detail. This is how they develop their opinions concerning others and about things in life. To put it another way, they are looking and listening when you least expect it. They are **"taking it all in"**.

In the final analysis, when divorce occurs and there are children involved, we owe it to them to keep them as our primary focus. Sowing positive seeds into their lives, to nurture and cultivate them for God's kingdom and for generations to come. Remember, God has a plan for their lives as well as yours, and the circumstances are just a link in the chain that will lead each of you to the destiny that God has ordained for you. On the condition that, He is allowed to lead you as you lead them.

CHAPTER *Three*

Single, Yet Married

IN THIS CHAPTER, I will discuss periods of singleness and being alone, while married to my former spouse. This will also include the time period, after the separation, prior to, and after the divorce. To emphasize, as a Christian woman, I become single after the divorce, yet married to the Lord Jesus Christ. Thus, single, yet married.

Alone, But Not Abandoned

During this time my former spouse moved out of our home and we became separated. So to better understand what was happening to me; I needed to define three words: alone, abandon, and lonely. First, the word alone is defined as being without other people or secluded from other people. Second, the word abandon is defined as to leave someone with no intention of returning. Third, the word lonely is defined as feeling distressed or sad when separated from other people. With these definitions in mind, I began to put my feelings into perspective and admitted that these words were operating in my life.

In other words, I was alone. And to be alone can cause you to feel lonely or abandoned. Therefore, as I entered a state of singleness, I had to condition my mind to start to think single. Even though the divorce was not legally final, another part of the divorce process was becoming a reality. Furthermore, the separation was most devastating for me. I had to learn how to live alone because I never actually lived alone without another adult in the household. I literally walked around in a state of dazedness for about three months. I felt blind-sided. The world seemed as if it was turned upside down and spinning out of control. I continually thought and said, **"Stop world and let me off!"**

Meanwhile, I felt so much shame and embarrassment because my spouse and I were both born again, spirit-filled Christians and in regular attendance in the local church. And prior to the separation, we held leadership positions in our former church. However, we were in the process of becoming another worldly statistic. I was so angry at the situation and knew the enemy was robbing us because my former spouse did not want to get help for the marriage. Besides, separation and divorce was not to be our reality.

After all, we were in a word-based ministry and should understand what God's word said about marriage. But that was not the case. We had Christian friends who believed that we could work out our differences and encouraged us to seek Godly counsel from our pastor and other pastor friends. And we finally received some counseling, but by this time it was too late.

The fact remained that my former spouse did not want to act on their advice, which was reconciliation. And now because of his refusal to take action towards reconciliation we were headed in the direction towards divorce. And my whole world seemed shattered into a million pieces all around me. I could not believe it. I asked myself, **"Was this a bad nightmare?"** No, I was wide awake and feeling the pain.

There were many days and nights I felt so lost because of the abandonment. But deep down in my heart I knew that I needed to be alone, so God could speak to and revive my heart. I can best describe this time of separation as a place of solitude and purging. Likewise, during this time, I did not communicate in great detail about what was going on with me personally with many people. There were a select number of people that came during different intervals into my life to help through prayer, fellowship, and friendship. Additionally, my family, church family, and children's school were a great support system.

Furthermore, this was a time in my Christian walk that I had to walk alone for the most part, and it provided opportunity for me to experience another aspect of God's glory. Those times of aloneness are set apart so we can see the provision of God and recognize that when total deliverance comes, it will only come through Him. Not to mention, no man will be able to say they did it all for you or had anything to add to the end results. Ordinarily, man can only go so far with us when we face devastating circumstances, before we realize the need for someone greater to help us with our situation. This is when God reveals Himself to us, so we can know that He is God and besides Him there is none other.

Even though, I was shaken by the many events transpiring, God was right there comforting me, and making sure that I had everything that I needed to survive the situation. I was abandoned by my former spouse, but not by God. And as time passed, God filled those places of abandonment and loneliness with His presence, and then I saw Jesus as my husband.

> *And thou shalt remember all the way which the Lord thy God led thee those forty years in the wilderness, to humble thee, and to prove thee, to know what was in thine heart, whether thou wouldest keep his commandments, or no.* **Deuteronomy 8:2 (KJV)**

> *For your maker is your husband— the Lord of Hosts is His Name— and the Holy One of Israel is your Redeemer; the God of the whole earth He is called.* **Isaiah 54:5**

Above all, God is the only one with us twenty-four hours in a day and three hundred sixty-five days of a year. He is there constantly throughout our lifetime. What great security we have in God!

> *"for He [God] Himself has said, I will not in any way fail you nor give you up nor leave you without support. [I will] not, [I will] not, [I will] not in any degree leave you helpless nor forsake nor let [you] down (relax My hold on you)! [Assuredly not!]".* **Hebrews 13:5b**

...and, lo, I am with you alway, even unto the end of the world. Amen **Matthew 28:20b (KJV)**

The State of Singleness

When the divorce became legally final; I had to face the fact that I was a Christian woman and divorced. This meant that I was no longer physically or legally married, but single. However, I was spiritually married to Christ. As an illustration of this spiritual marriage that occurred many years before when I accepted Christ as my Lord and Savior. I was spiritually baptized into the body of Christ by the Holy Spirit. As a result, I became a part of Christ's body, which is the church; His bride. When accepting Jesus as Lord and Savior; there is a covenant relationship (a union) created with God. Thus, every born-again believer is the bride of Christ and married to Him.

Because of this, I totally submitted myself to Him; mind, will, emotions, and body. In particular, my body, which is God's temple, and the dwelling place of the Holy Spirit. With attention to this, I truly made Him the Lord of my life. After submitting, He becomes the head, just as the husband is of the wife.

With any relationship there should be a foundation to establish its purpose. And that purpose should include fulfilling God's plan for our lives and to do that, we need to follow His lead. So when we are in our state of singleness we can learn that His ways are best. Therefore, Jesus Christ is that foundation to any present or future relationship that we should desire. Ultimately, when I commit to the principles of God's word and honor them, I give them the authority to guide my life.

In view of this, I found myself in desperate need of a rebuild (a full renovation); mentally as well as emotionally. Wounds were developed after being damaged in my emotions as well as my mind, and some were too deep to recognize off the surface. So this is when opportunity presented itself through those wounds for the Lord to show me those areas to improve and reveal the truth from His word to renew my mind and speak to my heart.

That is to say, God showered me with His abundant love and confirmed and affirmed me in Him. Making it clear to me that I was skillfully created by Him and that I had self-worth and that He had placed in me invaluable assets that needed to be nurtured, cultivated, and enhanced over time. I needed permanent change to occur in my heart so I could get back up again and recover from all that had happened. God built up my self-esteem and gave me confidence to believe again that life was worth pursuing for my children as well as for myself. Definitely, I needed this encouragement from Him.

After all, God desires every single Christian to be whole or complete in the knowledge of Him and who we are according to His word before we enter into a relationship and truly enhance another individual's life.

For no other foundation can anyone lay than that which is [already] laid, which is Jesus Christ (the Messiah, the Anointed One). **1Corinthians 3:11**

[15]Do you not see and know that your bodies are members (bodily parts) of Christ (the Messiah)? Am I therefore to take the parts of Christ and make [them] parts of a prostitute? Never! Never! [16]Or do you know and realize that when a man joins himself with a prostitute, he becomes one body with her? The two, it is written, shall become one flesh. [17] But the person who is united to the Lord becomes one spirit with Him. [18]Shun immorality and all sexual looseness [flee from impurity in thought, word, or deed]. Any other sin which a man commits is one outside the body, but he who commits sexual immorality sins against his own body. [19]Do you not know that your body is the temple (the very sanctuary) of the Holy Spirit Who lives within you, Whom you have received [as a gift] from God? You are not your own, [20]You were bought with a price [purchased with a preciousness and paid for, made His own]. So then, honor God and bring glory to Him in your body. **1 Corinthians 6:15-20**

I will praise thee; for I am fearfully and wonderfully made: marvelous are thy works: and that my soul knoweth right well. **Psalm 139:14 (KJV)**

A Love Relationship with God

In essence, my time of singleness was a bonding period with God; getting to know Him on a more personal basis as well as myself. Therefore, creating and cultivating a more intimate knowledge of Him. I perceived that the direction of my relationship with God was headed to a place that only He could carry me. I realized that there is only one way to really know one's self, and that begins with personally knowing God. And this knowledge of Him must be gained by entering into an intimate relationship with Him.

To begin this process of intimacy, I needed to enjoy alone time with God. I continually saturated myself in God's presence and His word. For example: listening to ministry tapes, reading many bible-based books on specific issues that I was dealing with, and being counseled by my pastor. And this is when the anointing of God destroyed yokes of bondages that I had acquired throughout the years, even some in childhood.

Likewise, there were times when I went shopping, out to lunch, dinner, or just quiet time spent alone with Him. Therefore, being content in Him and with Him created the desire to look to Him to supply all of my needs, desires, and wants. At that time He was my companion and friend. I could relate to Him because no one else really understood what I was going through and He knew every detail and all the specifics. He kept my inner most secrets as well as counseled me. He supernaturally filled every desire I had; I truly found Him to be a provider, comforter, encourager, but most of all a **"true gentleman"**. To point out that only God knows how to love my inner being. He created man and the soul. And for this reason, only He satisfies the soul.

> *And the Lord God formed man of the dust of the ground, and breathed into his nostrils the breath of life; and man became a living soul.* **Genesis 2:7 (KJV)**

> *For He satisfies the longing soul and fills the hungry soul with good.* **Psalm 107:9**

During the time I spent in communion with God, worshipping and sitting at His feet, I began to experience all He had for me; which included an abundance of His love, joy, peace, and goodness. Undoubtedly, these words describe God's presence, as well as exemplifies His Glory. To be in His presence is most rewarding and fulfilling. In other words, being with Him helped me to maintain balance in my life, kept me grounded, and with the right perspective. In fact, God is the only one who keeps me balanced, back then and even now.

Furthermore, those times of becoming more aware of my love relationship with God were priceless and cannot be compared to anything. Just to feel the love that God has for me is totally amazing and to understand that nothing can separate me from that love is beyond human comprehension, it must be spiritually discerned.

And it shall come to pass in that day, that his burden shall be taken away from off thy shoulder, and his yoke from off thy neck, and the yoke shall be destroyed because of the anointing. **Isaiah 10:27 (KJV)**

You will show me the path of life: in Your presence is fullness of joy, at Your right hand there are pleasures for evermore. **Psalm 16:11**

[35] Can anything ever separate us from Christ's love? Does it mean he no longer loves us if we have trouble or calamity, or are persecuted, or hungry, or destitute, or in danger, or threatened with death? [36] (As the scriptures say, "For your sake we are killed every day; we are being slaughtered like sheep.") [37] No, despite all these things, overwhelming victory is ours through Christ, who loved us. [38] And I am convinced that nothing can ever separate us from God's love. Neither death nor life, neither angels nor demons, neither our fears for today nor our worries about tomorrow — not even the powers of hell can separate us from God's love. [39] No power in the sky above or in the earth below— indeed, nothing in all creation will ever be able to separate us from the love of God that is revealed in Christ Jesus our Lord. **Romans 8:35-39 (NLT)**

A RESILIENT HEART

O taste and see that the Lord is good: **Psalm 34:8a (KJV)**

Overall, the Lord did marvelous things for me spiritually as well as materially. As a result, my attitude, personality, and perspectives changed. I began to see miraculous breakthroughs come as I continually submitted myself to the Holy Spirit and allowed Him to cover me in His grace. Then God placed me in the role that He desired for me; that of a virtuous woman.

¹⁰Who can find a virtuous woman? for her price is far above rubies. ¹¹ The heart of her husband trusts in her confidently and relies on and believes in her securely, so that he has no lack of [honest] gain or need of [dishonest] spoil. ¹²She comforts, encourages, and does him only good as long as there is life within her. ²²ᵇHer clothing is of linen, pure and fine, and of purple [such as that of which the clothing of priests and the hallowed cloths of the temple were made]. ²³Her husband is known in the [city's] gates, when he sits among the elders of the land. ²⁴She makes fine linen garments and leads others to buy them; she delivers to the merchants girdles [or sashes that free one up for service]. ²⁵Strength and dignity are her clothing and her position is strong and secure; she rejoices over the future [the latter day or time to come, knowing that she and her family are in readiness for it]! ²⁶She opens her mouth in skillful and godly Wisdom, and on her tongue is the law of kindness [giving counsel and instruction]. ²⁷She looks well to how things go in her household, and the bread of idleness (gossip, discontent, and self-pity) she will not eat. ²⁸Her children rise up and call her blessed (happy, fortunate, and to be envied); and her husband boasts of and praises her, [saying], ²⁹Many daughters have done virtuously, nobly, and well [with the strength of character that is steadfast in goodness], but you excel them all. ³⁰Charm and grace are deceptive, and beauty is vain [because it is not lasting], but a woman who reverently and worshipfully fears the Lord, she shall be praised! ³¹Give her of the fruit of her hands, and let her own works praise her in the gates [of the city]! **Proverbs 31:10-12…22b-31 (AMP & KJV)**

CHAPTER

Abundance and Restoration

Lessons Learned

THIS CHAPTER IS dedicated to reveal the lessons learned in order to move forward in a future marital relationship. Today many Christian singles are faced with instability and misguidance in four areas as relates to male-female relationships. I am speaking in regards to those relationships that have a purpose of courtship and then marriage, not mere dating. These four areas are: friendship, intimacy, courtship and marriage. They are interwoven and essentially interdependent upon each other. In fact, as I discuss them, it will be apparent. I experienced a breach or neglect in all those areas with my former spouse. They were improperly handled because of ignorance, neglect, and failing to be in agreement. And as a result, I experienced much pain, emotional distress, and disappointment.

These feelings were not something I wanted to base my future relationships on because I wanted to live without feeling all the pain. So I chose to believe that God would help me and replace the pain, emotional distress, and disappointment with abundance and restoration.

Furthermore, I needed to increase my faith. I had to do this in order to receive the abundance and restoration that God had for me. So one day I remembered the story of Job, and began to think and meditate about what happened to him. To paraphrase, Job was a man blessed of God and the enemy was allowed to come and destroy all of Job's possessions, including his health. In spite of all that happened with Job's circumstances, the pain and suffering he went through, God restored all that the enemy had stolen. So Job's story provided an illustration and testimony of how God can restore a life that was full of negative circumstances. This gave me hope and strength to believe and continue to trust God.

> *¹¹And the Lord shall guide you continually and satisfy you in drought and in the dry places and make strong your bones. And you shall be like a watered garden and like a spring of water whose waters fail not. ¹²And your ancient ruins shall be rebuilt; you shall raise up the foundations of [buildings that have laid waste for] many generations; and you shall be called Repairer of the Breach, Restorer of Streets to Dwell in.* **Isaiah 58:11-12**

> *.... I came that they may have and enjoy life, and have it in abundance (to the full, til it overflows).* **John 10:10b**

> *So then Faith cometh by hearing and hearing by the word of God.* **Romans 10:17**

> *10b.... also the Lord gave Job twice as much as he had before. 12aSo the Lord blessed the latter end of Job more than his beginning....* **Job 42:10b, 12a (KJV)**

The Neglect of Friendship

When I initially meet my former spouse I did not ask God if there was potential for this man to be my friend before I developed romantic feelings for him. This had nothing to do with him; it was all about how I had related to the aspect of friendship with men in past relationships. Friendship and romance just did not mix, mainly because I did not have a real understanding of true friendship when it came to male-female relationships. They were either all friends or all romance, no in between or combination of friendship/romance. For this reason, I could not see myself in a relationship that could begin in friendship, and then eventually lead to romance.

ABUNDANCE AND RESTORATION

The two just did not mix according to my viewpoint. Even though I heard throughout the years from family and friends, how they were friends first with the person they married. I never experienced such a luxury to develop a friendship before or after marriage with my former spouse.

Generally, developing a friendship is essential in building the foundation of a relationship. Yet, I did not put emphasis on friendship, nor biblical principles. Instead I focused more on worldly likes and dislikes which drew my attention to the physical attributes of my former spouse more than the things that truly matter, one being compatibility and the other being communication. In addition, let me point out that personality and character also play major roles in the compatibility and communication aspects of a friendship as well.

In other words, many aspects of each individual's character will be revealed in friendship and this will determine if there is compatibility between them. Incidentally, there was no compatibility between us and communication was neglected. From hindsight, we neglected to take time to become friends and rushed into a romantic relationship. This led me to emphasize in my mind how great it was to have his attention and be married to him.

After all, all of my closest friends were married and I felt left out. So, I truly was not establishing any type of foundation and if I would have been more God-seeking, I would have been able to develop a friendship first and proceeded with the relationship as God desired for me. But it was my decision to get into the relationship solely looking at romance rather than friendship. Therefore, I may have missed important areas in both our characters as well as personalities that needed to be examined closer.

If you are in a relationship today with a potential mate, it is imperative to think about this question: **"Has your soul been knit to another equally by God's guidance and power or have you unequally yoked yourself to another led by your power?"** I pray that the answer is the **"A"** portion of the question.

> *But every person is tempted when he is drawn away, enticed and baited by his own evil desire (lust, passions).* **James 1:14**

Friendship

A friendship is a relationship between individuals that is based on love, commitment, loyalty, and trust. A friend is considered to be one that you can share common interests; there is commonality. Each person keeping the others' well-being at the forefront; wanting to bless them with gifts, talents, and resources that God has bestowed upon their life. With this intention, you encourage and support one another and share truth with one another in any situation or circumstance. Friendship is important to God and it has good benefits.

> *And [so] the Scripture was fulfilled that says, Abraham believed in (adhered to, trusted in, and relied on) God, and this was accounted to him as righteousness (as conformity to God's will in thought and deed), and was called God's friend.* **James 2:23**

To develop a friendship with anyone, there must be an inner joy in being alone and truthful to one's self at all times, there is no room for pretense. We must have self-confidence before we can have a lasting and productive friendship with anyone. This self-confidence comes when we get to know God. Because getting to know the word of God will reveal to you who God is and who you are, and this will set the foundation to knowing others as well.

So, when a potential mate presents to us, the spiritual, personal connection we have already established with God will help us identify if this individual is truly born again or if we are to proceed forward with the relationship. Because we are able to hear God's voice and can trust Him to lead us. In other words, to have a personal relationship with God will enable us to be more sensitive to His leadership and guidance. And this will clear the path for Him to develop a friendship, if this is His plan for us and that potential mate.

For this reason, single Christians can have good God-ordained male-female friendships with a potential mate that can last into the marital union. After all, there is nothing that can compare to God's timing, because when

He knits our heart and soul to that special person of like faith; we then experience true friendship. And when God blesses us with it, we should honor Him by honoring the relationship.

Key elements of friendship:
- Each individual seeks the best interest of the other person
- Each individual is sensitive and responsive to the needs of the other person
- Each individual is eager to communicate with and shows concern for the other person
- Each individual gives encouragement and support to the other person

Do not be unequally yoked with unbelievers [do not make mismated alliances with them or come under a different yoke with them, inconsistent with your faith]. For what partnership have right living and right standing with God with iniquity and lawlessness? Or how can light have fellowship with darkness? **2 Corinthians 6:14**

A friend loves at all times, and is born, as is a brother, for adversity. **Proverbs 17:17**

A man that hath friends must show himself friendly: and there is a friend that sticketh closer than a brother. **Proverbs 18:24 (KJV)**

No one has greater love [no one has shown stronger affection] than to lay down (give up) his own life for his friends. **John 15: 13**

My sheep hear my voice, and I know them, and they follow me: **John 10:27(KJV)**

The Neglect of Intimacy

Generally speaking, when you have a relationship with someone there is a certain amount of closeness established between those involved. There is an emotional connection or bond. This connection or bond is established over time by verbal communication and spending time together. All things considered, over time intimacy is created between those involved. This was not the case between my former spouse and I, verbal communication was poor and spending quality time together was little to non- existent. I was not freely communicating or sharing myself emotionally and as a result there was no emotional closeness or intimacy. The communication was not heartfelt, neither was there emotional support. We really did not know or understand each other spiritually.

Consequently, we were estranged and had no realization of that fact. For the most part, we did not share our daily lives in a manner that caused us to grow and bond into that one flesh, which later will bring both into that place of agreement that is very much a necessity in the relationship between a husband and wife.

Intimacy

Intimacy is a word used by many to usually describe a sexual relationship between a male and a female. On the other hand, we should be reminded that this word could also be used to describe a close, personal relationship with God because learning how to be intimate with our spouse should begin with our relationship with Christ. There can be intimacy in any relationship without sexual involvement.

The word intimacy can take friendship to another level. When someone is your friend and there is intimacy between the two of you; the other person is more than just an acquaintance or associate. This is someone that you can share feelings, dreams, hopes, and the details of everyday life. They become a part of your emotional as well as mental space. There is an emotional connection or bond.

Granted, a friend may see many facets of your personality that others may not see, you can be real with them, and they are nonjudgmental. You are free to be yourself. In other words, a friend will allow you to be yourself without the expectation of performance. We don't have to audition or play a role; we win with them all the time. Whether, good, bad, or indifferent.

At times, too much commonality with our friends may abuse the relationship. Therefore, to keep the relationship without abuse we must continually assess ourselves and show love, respect, and be truthful to one another. Besides that, we must allow enough space for each individual to maintain their personal identity. In general, we should never try to control, manipulate, or suffocate another person's individuality; if this happens, it can lead to resentment and strife that may eventually end the relationship.

While this may be true, I do believe that we must hold our friends accountable and there must be mutual respect in the relationship. Just because there is a bond of closeness or intimacy does not mean that we can say or do anything that comes to mind without considering the feelings of that other person. As mentioned earlier, there must be love, respect, and truth shared to preserve the intimacy aspect of the relationship.

The Neglect of Courtship

When I initially met my former spouse we were not seeking God for a mate, so we definitely did not seek Him to see if it was His will that we were together. We went about the dating path just as the world encourages because this was common to us. In fact, there was no courtship involved before we were married. In other words, marriage was not our initial goal or purpose, nor the reason why we were together.

Obviously, in dating there may not be any guidelines or specifics as relates to the direction of the relationship stated up front. In this case, any direction is okay. On the contrary, for the Christian single this is not okay and we should not imitate the world's way of dating in any form or fashion. We must have purpose and vision for our relationships. First and foremost, God has given us a destiny to fulfill and we cannot do that if we are not following His divine plan.

Therefore, courtship always gives a purpose of marriage to the relationship, and dating may or may not have an intended purpose of marriage. As a result, dating can lead us in and out of relationships continually. For example, we get emotionally involved to later find out that this person is not the one, then on to the next person that you may be attracted to physically or emotionally. And those experiences tend to create an emotional roller coaster headed towards destruction. As a result, each time we date someone and get emotionally attached to them and things do not work out, seeds of mistrust and insecurity are planted in the mind and cause emotional baggage for future relationships.

Courtship

Courtship is the path for the Christian single to take as they consider marriage. Courtship is not dating. To explain, courtship is a period of time when couples seek God to determine if it is His will for them to marry each other. Courtship has purpose. Also, during the time of courtship we try to win the affection, emotions, and approval of another. We all want others to like us so we strive to make a good first impression. So, it is always important to remember, there is only one opportunity to meet someone for the first time. Automatically, during these times we put our best efforts to the front and suppress all our not so good qualities.

In reality, this is the time we need to bring the total package (the good and the bad) to the table of courtship. For instance, when we are rooted and grounded in who God has made us to be, it gives us the self-confidence we need to be ourselves. It produces freedom to trust God and know that He has created us with unique personalities; those that are likeable. And this fact provides us with the confidence to believe that we deserve good treatment from someone and that we are capable of giving good treatment in return.

Some ways to demonstrate good treatment to one another is by spending quality time together, verbally communicating, attending family, social and church activities, and obtaining pre-marital counseling from both individuals' pastors. Equally important, time spent alone should be limited and there should be mutually agreed upon guidelines and standards in place to deter placing oneself in sexually compromising situations, which may lead to fornication. For example, there should be limitations to phone conversations, physical contact, and how we dress when we are together. For the most part, courtship is not the time to cultivate a sexual relationship by

ABUNDANCE AND RESTORATION

trying to seduce or allure someone with words, actions, or dress.

Instead, courtship is where the friendship should be cultivated and nurtured. Sexual intimacy should be encountered after marriage. On the condition that God says to honor the marital bed. Because when two people join themselves sexually, bonds are developed in their souls and this uniting of souls was created by God for marriage.

> *[18]Shun immorality and all sexual looseness [flee from impurity in thought, word, or deed]. Any other sin which a man commits is one outside the body, but he who commits sexual immorality sins against his own body. [19]Do you know that your body is the temple (the very sanctuary) of the Holy Spirit, Who lives within you, Whom you have received [as a Gift] from God? You are not your own, [20]You are bought with a price [purchased with a preciousness and paid for, made His own]. So then, honor God and bring glory to Him in your body.* **1Corinthians 6:18-20**

> *Let marriage be held in honor (esteemed worth, precious, of great price and especially dear) in all things. And thus let the marriage bed be undefiled (kept undishonored); for God will judge and punish the unchaste [all guilty of sexual vice] and adulterous.* **Hebrews 13:4**

So, as a Christian single woman or man, we are not to live loose or carry ourselves in an ungodly manner when spending time with a potential mate during courtship. To emphasize, as a Godly woman I will be known by my conversation, mannerisms and wardrobe that exemplify Christ. I should be a capable, intelligent, virtuous woman. And because of this a Godly man will appreciate and respect a Godly woman's character, her inner beauty, and most of all her spirituality; the relationship she has with God. In a similar fashion, a Godly man should be known by his straightforwardness. In fact, a Godly man will immediately, in the beginning of the relationship make his intentions known to you; there will be no second guessing or game-playing. Also, he will show you respect by his tone of voice and his acts of chivalry. See, a Godly woman appreciates an honest, intentional man. One who knows how to state his intentions upfront and shows you respect. And that respect is visible by his words as well as his actions towards you. And finally, when their hearts are captured, and they say **"I DO"**, both will thank and praise God that they did it His way, and it was well worth the wait!

> *A capable, intelligent, and virtuous woman- who can find her? She is far more precious than jewels and her value is far above rubies or pearls.* **Proverbs 31:10**
>
> *He who finds a [true] wife finds a good thing and obtains favor from the Lord.* **Proverbs 18:22**

Remember, God has a plan for your future lives together. So allow Him to cultivate and nurture the relationship. During the courtship, we should take our time and use wisdom and listen to God. It is of utmost importance to seek God's guidance wholeheartedly when choosing a mate, not being governed by our own understanding or emotions, but by the Spirit of God. Therefore, allow God to do what He does best because He made the first couple and placed them together in the Garden of Eden. He saw what Adam needed and created Eve. So, when it comes to selecting a mate, we need to put our emotions to the back and let our spirits come to the front and lead. By doing this will influence us to make wise decisions after much prayer and listening to God.

> *[18]Now the Lord God said, It is not good (sufficient, satisfactory) that the man should be alone; I will make him a helper meet (suitable, adapted, complementary) for him. [22]And the rib or part of his side which the Lord God had taken from the man He built up and made into a woman, and He brought her to the man.* **Genesis 2:18, 22**

The Neglect of Marriage

As mentioned previously, when I initially meet my former spouse we were not seeking God for a mate, so we definitely did not seek Him to see

ABUNDANCE AND RESTORATION

if it was His will that we be joined in marriage. In that case, marriage was not our initial goal or purpose, nor the reason why we were together.

So, later into the relationship when it came to the thought of marriage, I became excited with the sole fact that I was going to be married. After all, most of my friends were already married and I felt left out. It was more about my feelings or how I felt emotionally. This way of thinking significantly influenced my decisions from that point forward. To say it another way, the process and the actual wedding day were more exciting than my commitment to having a Godly marriage with a man that was right for me.

To point out, feelings as well as emotions fluctuate with situations and circumstances. It is dangerous to make decisions in life or marriage governed totally by our feelings or emotions. Furthermore, our marital relationship started out without us receiving marriage counseling or considering the principles of God's word concerning marriage. For this reason, we were not able to see everything being pulled together according to God's plan for us because of the transforming power of the word.

In a roundabout way, we thought we were doing it God's way, believing that because we were Christians we were right, but actually we were not. We were doing it our way, which was according to our understanding, and in the end led to a recipe for destruction.

> *[5]Lean on, trust in, and be confident in the Lord with all your heart and mind and do not rely on your own insight or understanding. [6]In all your ways know, recognize, and acknowledge Him, and He will direct and make straight and plain your paths.* **Proverbs 3:5-6.**

> *There is a way which seems right to a man and appears straight before him, but at the end of it is the way of death.* **Proverbs 14:12**

Also, we expected more from one another than we were able to give. Therefore, unrealistic expectations were placed on us and we were frequently disappointed. By the same token, we did know how to respond favorably to that which we could give. And it was not enough to keep us together.

On the positive side, it was unrealistic for me to think that I or my spouse will feel the exact same way continuously throughout the marriage or that my spouse will be the same in five, ten, fifteen years as they were when we first married.

Now, I understand that I must allow for adjustments over time. And this is where we need balance and wisdom from God in order to take each other at face value. Then we can love, respect, and appreciate one another in the place we are at in that particular moment. As with any relationship there are challenges that may occur and we must possess more than our feelings to sustain us, we must have commitment. And that commitment is first, to God, and then, one another.

Marriage

God created and ordained the marital union as sacred. As an illustration, two separate individuals stand before God, our betrothed, and the minister, we symbolize and declare and decree that we have come into agreement to connect our lives together and desire to become one flesh in the eyes God. And because of this, there is a spiritual-soul connection that occurs between the three. We honor God when we marry because He is the author and creator of the original marriage performed between Adam and Eve in the Garden of Eden. Additionally, marriage is a covenant between the husband, wife, and God that should be honored and cherished by both parties until that union is broken by death.

> *[22]And the rib or part of his side which the Lord God had taken from the man He built up and made into a woman, and He brought her to the man. [23]Then Adam said, This [creature] is now bone of my bones and flesh of my flesh; she shall be called Woman, because she was taken out of a man. [24]Therefore a man shall leave his father and his mother and shall become united and cleave to his wife, and they shall become one flesh.* **Genesis 2:22-24**
>
> *Let marriage be held in honor (esteemed worthy, precious, of great price, and especially dear) in all things. And thus let the*

marriage bed be undefiled (kept undishonored); for God will judge and punish the unchaste [all guilty of sexual vice] and adulterous. **Hebrews 13:4**

Above all, as Christians we should have a solid foundation before we commit to marriage. Namely, that foundation is a committed and intimate relationship with Jesus Christ. We must first come to the knowledge of our completeness in Him before entering into a marital relationship, and making a commitment to one another. This is to say, we must be proactive and commit ourselves, our spouse, and our marriage to the Lord.

Specifically, when each individual commits to God and one another, this will set the marriage up for success and create a bond like none other; to be interwoven with the *"Author"* of romance and the *"Creator"* of you and your spouse, what a beautiful partnership! Consequently, the marital union turns into that threefold cord that cannot be broken or easily severed. Given these facts, part of the ingredients in the recipe for marriage success is honoring God in your hearts and in the marriage. And when this is done, He will make sure that it stands the test of time.

Commit your way to the Lord [roll and repose each care of your load on Him]; trust (lean on, rely on, and be confident) also in Him and He will bring it to pass. **Psalms 37:5**

And though a man might prevail against him who is alone, two will withstand him. A threefold cord is not quickly broken. **Ecclesiastes 4:12**

Foundational principles of marriage:
- Marriage is a covenant relationship between a man, a woman, and God. He performed the first marriage in the Garden of Eden between Adam and Eve. **Genesis 2:22**

- Marriage is honorable and truly to be cherished in the eyes of God. Both, husband and wife being faithful to one another. **Hebrews 13:4**

- God uses marriage (the union between a man and his wife) as an analogy of the relationship between the church and His son Jesus; the church as the Bride of Christ. **Revelation 19:7-9**

- Be accountable to one another out of honor and respect to God. **Ephesians 5:21**

- Wives should submit to their husbands as unto the Lord, cooperate with and respect him. **Ephesians 5:22**

- Husbands should take their rightful place (of leadership) as the head of the wife, guiding her and protecting her. **Ephesians 5:23**

- Wives should be under the leadership (guidance) of their husbands in all things, just as the church is unto Christ. **Ephesians 5:24**

- Husbands should love their wives just as Christ loved the church and gave up His life for her. **Ephesians 5:25**

- Husbands should dwell with their wives according to knowledge and understanding, being considerate. **1 Peter 3:7**

When we respect and follow God's principles of marriage, there is order, harmony, peace, and fulfillment. To demonstrate, when God is the head of the man, then the man can take his rightful place as the covering of his wife. Then the wife can truly submit to her husband. Certainly, this is God's order. And God is about things done decently and in order.

> *⁶But from the beginning of creation God made them male and female. ⁷For this reason a man shall leave [behind] his father and his mother and be joined to his wife and cleave closely to her permanently. ⁸And the two shall become one flesh.* **Mark 10:6-8**
>
> *Let all things be done decently and in order.* **1 Corinthians 14:40 (KJV)**

ABUNDANCE AND RESTORATION

In the same way, when each spouse has knowledge, understands, and functions in their God appointed roles, this provides that order that God has established for marriage. Words cannot explain the feeling of elation in the heart and mind of a husband and his wife when this occurs. Truly, this is that secret place of peace and tranquility in God's will for the marital union. And this pleases Him.

With this in mind, communication is vital to the success of any relationship. But in marriage, there must be a balance maintained between the husband and wife as it relates to God and communication. Each individual must cultivate their personal relationship with God in order to know when and what to communicate to one another. Since God is all knowing we should follow His lead, and then we will learn how to communicate appropriately with our spouse. Take the time to learn one another so we can continue to grow into that oneness or **"one flesh"** that is meant for the marital union by God. To point out, God puts emphasis on the fact that the husband should dwell with his wife according to knowledge. He should study her and learn all he can about her, so she will in turn be able to respond positively to him.

Furthermore, as the marriage progresses and each individual continues to cultivate their personal relationship with God their marital relationship will grow and develop that **"one flesh"** (minding the same things and relating to one another on one accord; mentally, emotionally, and spiritually). Basically, coming into agreement with one another and this becomes fertile ground to plant seeds that will eventually blossom into marriage success.

Altogether, the areas of friendship, intimacy and courtship have a tremendous effect on marital success. They are interwoven and essentially interdependent upon each other. We cannot talk about one without overlapping, or talking about some aspects of the other.

Generally, we all dream about or have some unrealistic idea of what a perfect spouse or a perfect marriage should look like. On the contrary, there is no perfect spouse or perfect marriage. That is to say, we all have character flaws, weaknesses and incompleteness in ourselves. In the final analysis, we are only complete in Jesus Christ, and He is the reference point that we should use to keep balance in our relationships, in regards to the areas of friendship, intimacy, courtship, and marriage.

He Restores My Soul

Actually, I truly loved my former spouse and wanted the marriage to work. However, when we look to other people to find happiness, we set ourselves up for heartache. And when we can't find that happiness in those people, we become disappointed or hurt. This is what happened to me. In fact, during the marriage I was looking to my former spouse to provide me with total happiness and giving him a place in my heart that was not his from the beginning. Now, I realize that God should have been in that place. Besides, no man, which includes your spouse, can fill that place in your heart that is only reserved for God.

When two people are joined in the union of marriage, soul ties are developed and when separation or divorce occurs, there is a disruption in the soul, a tearing away. As an illustration, it feels as if someone has actually torn or snatched a piece of your flesh without using any type of anesthetic to suppress the pain. During the process of the divorce, I was so out of touch with reality and hurt flooded my soul beyond anything that I thought could be described. Divorce creates a very painful wound in the soul and can leave scars on your soul that may affect future relationships.

To explain, man has a soul and it is comprised of the mind, will and emotions. And when one or all of these areas are wounded you experience pain, sorrow, agony, and grief. You simply go into a period of mourning. I experienced so much emotional instability; I needed a cure for this soul thing that was happening to me. At this point, there was no man-made cure for what I was going through.

Frequently, man will offer various strategies and techniques to take you from one step to the next, but for the most part, they are only temporary fixes. But I needed immediate relief as well as a permanent cure for this condition in my soul. See, I was broken in my mind, my will, and my emotions, and it seemed like that brokenness was beyond repair. Not to mention, the circumstance of divorce could have taken me emotionally and mentally to a place of no return. I became fearful that every man that I would meet would forsake, hurt, or betray me as my former spouse had; and that was not something that I wanted to go back through again. I went through a period of distrust and could not mentally see myself in any relationship with any man for approximately four years after the divorce.

Looking back, I allowed myself to agonize over my situation much too long. I really didn't put my total trust in God. I was looking at my circumstances and reliving the events of what had happened to me before and during the divorce. Also, allowing others to keep those events alive during frequent discussions and conversations.

Occasionally, we may feel as if we can face certain circumstances in our lives with dependence on our knowledge and endurance. Unfortunately, each time this is not the case. We must have faith in God and trust Him, because He is the only guaranteed way in which we can see the power of restoration work in our circumstances.

From that point forward, I had to rely on God for the cure I needed, and embrace the fact that Jesus is the **"Healer"** and only He can heal a broken heart and restore the soul.

I can only describe my deliverance as a process. And that process revealed and acquainted me with myself and what God desired for me to have in a marital relationship. In my situation, the Holy Spirit led and showed me the need to renew my mind in the area of marriage. I began to have a desire to know biblical principles in God's word concerning marriage. This opened the door for me to make a conscious decision to rise above the hurt and look to God for healing and restoration.

With this in mind, I recognized three important facts prior to the six steps I took in order to receive the deliverance and restoration God had for me. One, I must let go of the past in order to move forward with the future. Two, I must get my focus and my words off of the current situation and put my focus and words on what I believe my future situation will be, and start to speak it out loud and on purpose. Three, I must keep my spirit strong with the word of God and not allow my circumstances or feelings to sway my faith in the word of God, which is my hope.

A RESILIENT HEART

> ....but this one thing I do, forgetting those things which are behind, and reaching forth unto those things which are before, ... **Philippians 3:13b**

> *Faith is the confidence that what we hope for will actually happen; it gives us assurance about things we cannot see.* **Hebrews 11:1 (NLT)**

> *For we walk by faith, not by sight:* **2 Corinthians 5:7**

> *But without faith it is impossible to please and be satisfactory to Him. For whoever would come near to God must [necessarily] believe that God exists and that He is a rewarder of those who earnestly and diligently seek Him [out].* **Hebrews 11:6**

Six steps that I took in order to receive the deliverance and restoration God had for me.

1. **Acknowledged** that there was a problem/need to myself and God

2. **Believed** that God can and will help me

3. **Asked** God to help me

4. **Received** help from God

5. **Followed** God's instructions for me

6. **Walked in** total deliverance by renewing my mind continually with God's word and doing what the Holy Spirit told me to do

> ¹*The Lord is my shepherd; I shall not want,*²*He maketh me to lie down in green pastures: he leadeth me besides the still waters.*³*He restoreth my soul....* **Psalm 23: 1-3a (KJV)**

> ²⁵*And I will restore to you the years that the locust hath eaten, the cankerworm, and the caterpillar, and the palmerworm, my great army which I sent among you.* ²⁶*And ye shall eat in plenty, and be ssatisfied, and praise the name of the Lord your God,that*

ABUNDANCE AND RESTORATION

hath dealt wondrously with you: and my people shall never be ashamed. **Joel 2:25-26 (KJV)**

He heals the brokenhearted and binds up their wounds [curing their pains and sorrow]. **Psalm 147:3**

[14]And this is the confidence (the assurance, the privilege of boldness) which we have in Him: [we are sure] that if we ask anything (make any request) according to His will (in agreement with His own plan), He listens to and hears us. [15]And if (since) we [positively] know that He listens to us in whatever we ask, we also know [with settled and absolute Knowledge] that we have [granted us as our present possessions] the requests made of Him. **1 John 5:14-15**

Eventually, God helped me to change my way of thinking. And this had to occur if I will one day in the future trust a man again in marriage. Simply to say, my focus or thinking was now in the right direction. Therefore, I did not feel the desire to group all men into a category that they would intentionally betray or hurt me. And I started to believe that I could trust a man in the manner that could lead to a committed, successful marital union in the future.

As I look back, with great **gratitude**, I can undoubtedly say, it was God who restored my **soul** and caused healing to flow through my heart. And because of this, I have seen God's sustaining power. **I would not have made it without Him!** He was, is, and continues to be my help, my strength, my comforter, my provider, my happiness, my joy, my friend…..**MY ALL!**

In the day when I called, You answered me; and You strengthened me with strength (might and flexibility to temptation) in my inner self. **Psalm 138:3**

For I will restore health to you, and I will heal your wounds, says the Lord;… **Jeremiah 30:17a**

A RESILIENT HEART

> *Instead of your [former] shame you shall have a twofold recompense; instead of dishonor and reproach [your people] shall rejoice in their portion. Therefore in their land they shall possess double [what they had forfeited]: everlasting joy shall be theirs.* **Isaiah 61:7**

> *And after you have suffered a little while, the God of all Grace [Who imparts all blessing and favor], Who has called you to His [own] eternal glory in Christ Jesus, will Himself complete and make you what you ought to be, Establish and ground you securely, strengthen, and settle you.* **1 Peter 5:10**

Reunited

There is power in togetherness. There is power in unity. There is power in agreement. See, God created man as a triune being, after His image, and man is comprised of a body, a soul, and a spirit. Man was originally created so that the soul and spirit would function harmoniously together. When God blew the breath of life into Adams nostrils, he became a living soul. The disharmony between the soul and spirit came when sin entered into the earth because of the transgression of Adam and Eve in the Garden of Eden.

With this in mind, Power is created when the soul is reunited with the spirit. See, the Spirit of God, the Holy Spirit dwells in the born-again spirit of man. Even more, there is a great peace and harmony you obtain when you become in agreement with the Creator of the universe. To explain, I was now allowing my spirit to take charge of my soul (mind, my will, and my emotions). And as a result, my thoughts and my actions began to line up with the word of God. This is when my soul was reunited with my spirit. And then they became in harmony. See, your spirit has the desire for wholeness and togetherness because that is the nature of God and the spirit of man is where He dwells. And it always wants to do the will of God.

Therefore, when we are going through heartbreak and devastating circumstances that we think we cannot recover from, it is important to realize that God is waiting and willing to help. Therefore, it is of utmost importance for our soul to become in agreement with our spirit, because this will play a vital role in what type of outcome we will experience.

To put it another way, when we allow the spirit man to be in charge of our thoughts and action; we are not, at that point giving our soul or our natural man (soul/flesh) authority to take charge of our thoughts and actions. Although this is true, we must remember that there is a continual war between the spirit and the soul, and we must continually keep the soul in check. Besides, if we don't put it in check, it will take us captive by our thoughts, feelings, and emotions.

> *^{26a} And God said, Let us make man in our image, after our likeness: ^{27a}So God created man in his own image, in the image of God created he him;* **Genesis 1:26a, 27a**

> *And the Lord God formed man of the dust of the ground, and breathed into his nostrils the breath of life, and man became a living soul.* **Genesis 2:7 (KJV)**

> *The sinful nature wants to do evil, which is just the opposite of what the Spirit wants. And the Spirit gives us desires that are opposite of what the sinful nature desires. These two forces are constantly fighting each other, so you are not free to carry out your good intentions.* **Galatians 5:17**

> *Casting down imaginations, and every high thing that exalteth itself against the knowledge of God, and bringing into captivity every thought to the obedience of Christ;* **2 Corinthians 10:5 (KJV)**

I can personally attest to the restoring power of God. The best way that I can describe what the Lord has done for me, is to say that He has taken the brokenness, pain, hurt, and distress that I felt in my soul and replaced it with wholeness, comfort, healing, and joy! The fact is that my soul has been reunited with my spirit, which gives much peace and harmony.

Throughout my entire disruptive relationship experience with separation and divorce, God tremendously blessed me spiritually. Certainly, my relationship with Him, my children, and others are the better for it.

Ultimately, the spiritual blessings that God has allowed me to experience has given me an inner strength which I did not have before and a more intimate, personal awareness of who the God of abundance and restoration is to me.

Up to the present moment, He has given me many spiritual blessings that can only be humanly explained to a certain point. To illustrate, He has swept me off my feet! You may ask, **"How has God swept you off your feet?"** My answer is, **"By being God, the perfect gentleman, the best friend, companion, lover of the soul, and confidant that a woman could ever have in her life!"** *He is breathtaking!*

Undoubtedly, I have found what *"true love"* means and how it feels because it comes from God. And as I continue to move forward with God, regardless of my situations or circumstances, I realize that God is faithful and He can give the substance and inner fortitude needed to possess **"A Resilient Heart"**. For this reason, I look forward to the future with hope and excitement, knowing that God has an ordained path for my life concerning friendship, intimacy, courtship and marriage.

> *⁴Love is patient and kind. Love is not jealous or boastful or proud ⁵or rude. It does not demand its own way. It is not irritable, and it keeps no record of being wronged. ⁶It does not rejoice about injustice but rejoices whenever the truth wins out. ⁷Love never gives up, never loses faith, is always hopeful, and endures through every circumstance.* **1Corinthians 13:4-7 (NLT)**

> *²So I have looked upon You in the sanctuary to see Your power and Your glory. ³Because Your loving☐ kindness is better than life, my lips shall praise You. ⁴So will I bless You while I live; I will lift up my hands in Your name. ⁵My whole being shall be satisfied as with morrow and fatness; and my mouth shall praise You with joyful lips. ⁶When I remember You upon my bed and meditate on You in the night watches. ⁷For you have been my help, and in the shadow of Your wings will I rejoice.* **Psalm 63:2-7**

The Lord will give [unyielding and impenetrable] strength to His people with peace. **Psalm 29:11**

Behold, I am the Lord, the God of all flesh; is there anything too hard for me? **Jeremiah 32:27**

Know, recognize and understand therefore that the Lord your God, He is the faithful God, Who keeps covenant and steadfast love and mercy with those who love Him and keep His commandments, to a thousand generations. **Deuteronomy 7:9**

Reflections

Reflections

Reflections

About the Author

Gwendolyn is a bible teacher, entrepreneur and motivational speaker, who currently resides in Shreveport, Louisiana. She grew up in a Christian household. However, she never experienced the victory that comes when one has a personal relationship with Jesus Christ.

In 1994, she became aware that she did not have this personal relationship with Jesus Christ and accepted that fact. Then she began to study and learn the scriptures. This is when she received revelation knowledge and understanding of the word of God that she now applies to everyday life.

As a result, this has made the difference in her life, which enables her to share with and teach others the truth and miraculous power of God's word with simplicity and authority.

www.ingramcontent.com/pod-product-compliance
Lightning Source LLC
Chambersburg PA
CBHW051715040426
42446CB00008B/905